WITH FLYING COLORS

Color Idioms
(A Multicultural Book)

By Anneke Forzani

Illustrated by Dmitry Fedorov

Language Lizard
Basking Ridge

For English audio and resources for teaching idioms,
see the last page of this book.

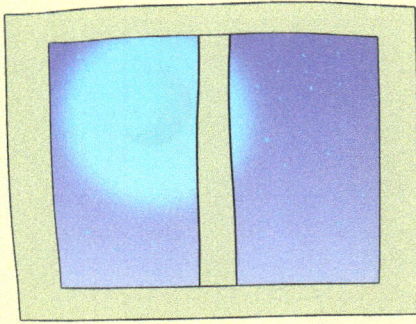

WHAT IS AN IDIOM?

An idiom is a phrase that says one thing but means something different. An idiom can be a quick way of saying something complicated. Knowing idioms will help you to understand and speak English fluently. This book contains idioms about colors.

SHOW YOUR TRUE COLORS

Meaning: Show what you really believe, show your true character

You **showed your true colors** when you asked the new student to sit with you.

TICKLED PINK

Meaning: To be delighted

Our mom was **tickled pink** when we gave her a new hat.

GREEN THUMB

Meaning: Having a talent for growing plants

My mother has a **green thumb,** so we always have fresh vegetables.

OUT OF THE BLUE

Meaning: Something happens unexpectedly

When I fell, my friend arrived **out of the blue** and made me feel better.

ROSE-COLORED GLASSES

Meaning: Seeing things in a positive light, being idealistic

He was so excited to visit the city that he saw everything through rose-colored glasses.

GOLDEN OPPORTUNITY

Meaning: An excellent opportunity that does not happen often

I had a **golden opportunity** to take lessons with an expert musician.

FEELING BLUE

Meaning: Feeling sad

I'm **feeling blue** because my best friend moved far away.

WHITE LIE

Meaning: A lie one tells so as not to hurt someone's feelings

I said a **white lie** when I told my friend that I liked her shoes.

ON A SILVER PLATTER

Meaning: To receive something without any effort or work

She has no chores and her parents give her everything **on a silver platter.**

RED HANDED

Meaning: Caught in the act of doing something wrong

We saw the chocolate on his face and caught him **red handed**.

ONCE IN A BLUE MOON

Meaning: Something that happens very rarely

My grandmother bakes lotus blossom cookies once in a blue moon.

GIVE THE GREEN LIGHT

Meaning: To give someone permission to do something

My parents **gave the green light** for us to go to the beach.

ROLL OUT THE RED CARPET

Meaning: To welcome someone with great hospitality

My mother **rolled out the red carpet** when her boss came to visit.

WITH FLYING COLORS

Meaning: To accomplish something almost perfectly

She completed the gymnastics routine with flying colors.

Visit **www.LanguageLizard.com/Color-Idioms** for additional resources for teaching and learning English idioms, including:

- English audio of this book
- Multicultural lesson plans for use in the classroom or at home
- Information on the origin of the idioms in this book
- Additional color idioms with their meaning, usage, and origin
- Information on idiom translations and idioms in other languages

This book is part of the **Language Lizard Idiom Series**.

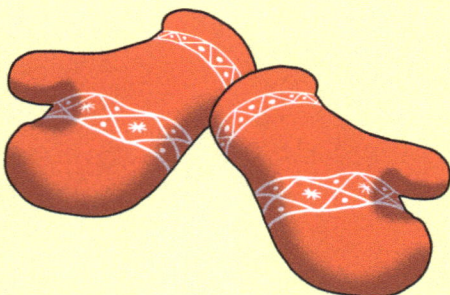

Visit **www.LanguageLizard.com** for a complete listing of the titles in this series and available languages.

www.ingramcontent.com/pod-product-compliance
Lightning Source LLC
Chambersburg PA
CBHW060902090426
42738CB00025B/3496